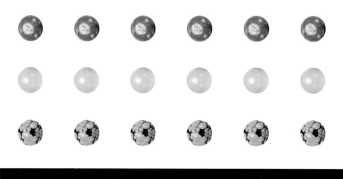

PRAYER ● BEADS

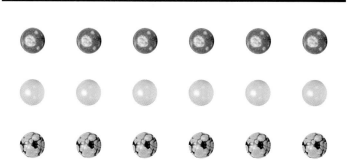

MANUELA DUNN MASCETTI • PRIYA HEMENWAY

Viking Compass

VIKING COMPASS
Published by the Penguin Group
Penguin Putnam Inc., 375 Hudson Street,
New York, New York 10014, U.S.A.
Penguin Books Ltd, 27 Wrights Lane,
London W8 5TZ, England
Penguin Books Australia Ltd, Ringwood,
Victoria, Australia
Penguin Books Canada Ltd, 10 Alcorn Avenue,
Toronto, Ontario, Canada M4V 3B2
Penguin Books (N.Z.) Ltd, 182–190 Wairau Road,
Auckland 10, New Zealand

Penguin Books Ltd, Registered Offices:
Harmondsworth, Middlesex, England

First published in 2001 by Viking Compass,
a member of Penguin Putnam Inc.

1 3 5 7 10 8 6 4 2

ISBN 0-670-03010-4

CIP data available

This book is printed on acid-free paper.∞

Printed in Malaysia
Set in Garamond
Produced by The Book Laboratory
Designed by i4 design | Sausalito, CA

CONTENTS

Part Three:

INTRODUCTION

I was in my early twenties when I arrived in India. Wearing a set of Indian prayer beads (a mala) *around my neck and carrying a slip of paper with a name scribbled on it, feeling both terribly alone and somewhat taken care of, I stepped down off the plane. I had no idea what I was doing in India, but with one hand clutching at the* mala, *and the other grasping my bag, I simply trusted. The* mala *had been given to me a few months before, and it had brought me to the beginning of what was to become a very special journey. I was unprepared for the events that were to unfold, and little did I know at the time that the* mala *I had been given was a tool of tremendous significance. To wear one is to acknowledge an inner state of surrender, a devotion to the journey of exploring oneself. (In traditional Hinduism and Buddhism, a* mala *is a set of beads used to count prayers. A deeper sense of their use is in the inexplicable relationship of the seeker to the path of awakening.)*

At the time, my mala *quickly became an outward reminder of an inner spiritual space. I was not presented with the technique, as many people are, of counting prayers or meditations upon the beads. Nor was I presented with its symbology. It was a gift and I had received it with tremendous gratitude. In my mind it was something of a good luck charm. I grasped it in my hand when something new, overwhelming, or strange began to happen; and I associated it* with the magic of good fortune. I think in some respect I gave the beads more credit than they deserved, but in another way it was due to their uncanny nature of recondite or esoteric support that I experienced the extraordinary beginnings of my own spiritual journey.

From those early days I continued to wear my *mala* for many years. In all my ups and downs, as I have moved through the many different phases of my life, my *mala* has been a constant. I would put it on in the morning and remember something sacred about myself. I would take it off at night and see in the beads an aspect of myself that would not die. Next to my skin or on top of my clothes, the beads thumped on my chest when I danced and hung quietly when I prayed.

By now my beads are charged with the stories of many years. While I no longer wear them every day, I keep them close and touch them often. During recent years I have learned a lot about their significance as a tool and an aid to prayer, which gives them a life of their own. Prayer beads, whether they are the *Hindu or Buddhist* mala, *the Muslim* tasbih, *or the Christian* rosary, have been used for hundreds of years as a tool for remembering. Remembering a prayer, remembering a mantra, repeating and remembering. Remember to respect, remember to love, remember to be true.

I was very young when I first put my prayer beads on, and although I had no idea why I was wearing them, they felt right. I was in love with the mysterious then as I am now, and they were a link to a door through which

I desperately wanted to walk. My experience of using them is an experience of an ever-deepening movement toward inner peace, and it is a great joy to me to acknowledge the spirit in which the beads were given to me.

It was suggested to me when I was young that I try hard to remember myself, that I try to remember that life is a prayer. It was suggested that I remember to sing and to dance; because one thing is sure: a prayerful heart is a grateful and joyful one. And so I have learned that life is more mysterious than measurable, and that those who live in the poetry, the song, the dance of prayer, are—and always have been—the blessed ones. The beads in the box that you have just opened come to you as an invitation to enter the prayerful space of joy.

Part One:

THE MYSTICAL FUNCTION OF PRAYER BEADS

The bead was first recognized, thousands of years ago, by the very earliest of humans, as an object that had a very special relationship with the world of the spirit. As amulets, talismans, charms, gifts, or symbolic adornments; whether made of seed, nut, shell, bone, wood, gem, or glass; beads were worn because they were felt to contain some mysterious, magical link between the world we can see and the world we cannot.

For millennia, living in accord with nature meant that all life was sacred. Everything, from the simple acts of eating and sleeping to more complex rituals of hunting and healing, had prayer as an essential aspect. Prayer is a state of surrender, a letting-go to the Gods, or to the way of existence. The relationship between prayer and prayer beads is ancient and mystical, and it forms the basis for this book.

THE VENERABLE BEAD

*O*ur English word "bead" comes from the Old English word *bede*, which means "prayer," or *bidden*, "to pray." It is related to the ancient Sanskrit *bodh* or enlightenment.

The most ancient Sanskrit name for prayer beads is *smarani*, which means "remembrancer." More commonly they were called *japamala*, or "muttering beads." *Japa* means "repetition," and *mala* is the word for a string of beads that also means "a garland of flowers."

Muslims call their prayer beads *tasbih*, which means "to praise God." It also means "reciter." The name Muslims use for touching the *tasbih* is *zikr*, or "remembrance."

Early Christian rosaries were called Paternosters (*pater* means "father" and *noster* means "our") because they were used in repetitions of the Lord's Prayer that begins with the words "Our Father." The English word "patter," meaning quick or glib speech, derives from paternoster. The word "rosary" stems from "rose garden," carrying the sense of garden or garland of prayers.

The word that the Tibetan lamas use for their use of beads, *trengwa*, means to purr like a cat—an organic drone that releases the mind into detachment.

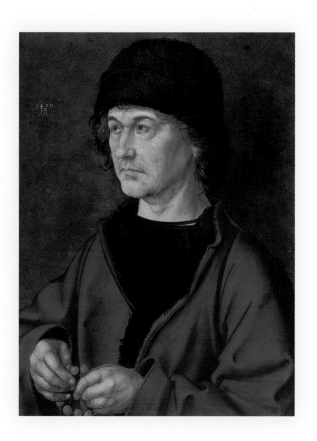

W H A T   A R E   P R A Y E R   B E A D S ?

*P*rayer beads are strands of beads used specifically for prayer. The nature of the prayer and the particular ways the strands are used are various, but the beads and the strands onto which they have been threaded have an ancient mystical significance. The beads themselves are usually chosen with their iconographic significance in mind, and it is perhaps because of this that they are able to represent and hold the space where the great mysteries of life and death become available. Lois Sherr Dubin in her book *The History of Beads from 30,000 B.C. to the Present* tells us: "It is perhaps through the use of rosaries, circlets of prayer beads, that people have achieved their most profound and complete relationship with beads."

Any bead that is used for prayer takes on a personal meaning far beyond its inherent beauty. Whether it is used as an amulet, a charm, or for prayer, the specific seeds, wood, or stones that are used have some mysterious capacity to transform. Whether this quality lies in the mythological or the scientific is hard to tell. But the element that gives a prayer bead meaning grows stronger with use.

The number of beads and the way they are worn differs from religion to religion, from one tradition to another, and from one intention or purpose to another. Some people wear their beads around the neck; others wear them on the wrist. Some carry them in a pouch or in a pocket or tie them onto the waist. Some keep them nearby, on a shelf

or altar, or in a box. Some have many sets of beads; some have only one.

The specific ways that prayer beads are used are as various as their configuration. Along with their effect as talisman, charm, or amulet goes their ability to protect and influence circumstances outside of the individual's control.

Then of course, there are the different methods of prayer itself. Webster's English dictionary explains prayer as a state or an act of addressing God. We could say, therefore that prayer beads are used to access a certain state of being. Counting prayers while fingering beads is a universal use. The idea behind this lies in the nature of repetition that soothes like a lullaby. It is calming and introspective. Beads are also used in prayer with a sense of beseeching or asking, thus making prayer more proactive.

Because we have essentially forgotten who we really are, and because the need to know is so compelling, techniques, meditations, and prayers abound. The most compelling reason for using beads in prayer is that they are a physical, tangible reminder of the state of divinity we have been born into.

PRAYING WITH YOUR BEADS

There is an anonymous account by a nineteenth-century Russian pilgrim (*The Way of a Pilgrim*, translated by H.M. French) that tells of the use of prayer beads. This pilgrim undertook his quest in the form of a spiritual journey, and at the beginning he was given a knotted woolen rosary by an old monk and told: "To start with you will say the Jesus Prayer three thousand times a day." The Jesus Prayer is another name for the "Lord's Prayer."

After two days the pilgrim found that repeating the prayer "became so easy and likable" that as soon as he stopped he felt "a sort of need to go on." After some time he began to lose all desire to do anything else. He often found himself repeating it in his sleep, he would dream of it at night and in the morning would wake to the sound of it.

In time he found pain vanished and any sense of anger or injury dissolved. He floated along in joyous detachment, wanting nothing but to be always alone and to pray without ceasing. Eventually he ceased verbal repetitions of the prayer, for the words were spoken in the depths of his heart, pounding to the tune of his heartbeat. The pilgrim reports that he found himself in a sublime state of "freedom from fuss."

This same state is what Buddhists, Hindus, Christians, and Muslims all practice as they use their beads. It is a state we all know but which, for the most part, we forget. It is a state in which we are free to experience our essential being, a state of great benediction in which we have access to God, or eternity, or bliss.

The most remarkable benefit that arises from the use of prayer beads is a remembrance of the divine. In remembering our divinity, we become free. We disentangle ourselves from the gravity of seriousness and we become lighter, happier, more detached from the problems and perplexities of our human condition. We may find we do not need to know why, or how, this happens. For some, being "free from fuss" is much like riding a bicycle—a knack learned through simple repetition. Prayer beads are most often used in conjunction with a prayer, a meditation, or a mantra.

WHAT IS PRAYER?

When the mind knows, we call it knowledge.
When the heart knows, we call it love.
When the being knows, we call it prayer.
—*Osho*

Prayer is communion and it happens in our interiority; it is the language of our soul and our connection with the divine. Prayer can be set into words, it can be sung or danced, it can be drummed or hammered, or it can be enjoyed like the fragrance of a rose. Prayer can be a wordless silence or an explosion of feeling, an act of love or a chore. Prayer can thank, praise, beseech, or cry, it can reject or acknowledge, for prayer takes many forms and is different for everyone. It is the continual reflection of our outer actions on the inner landscape of our being.

The forms of prayer are many. It can be practiced in stillness or activity, for a moment at a time or for long periods; it can be part of a ritual or it can be totally spontaneous. Prayer moves you out of your mind and into your heart, your being. It is a doorway through which you pass in order to connect with the sacred in yourself.

To enter the state of prayer, you can begin with a few words that touch your heart in some way, but remember, too, that prayer often begins unexpectedly in some ecstatic moment—beholding the beauty of nature or the silence of deep love. As a practice, prayer can be any ritual or activity that provides a way to move out of the head and into

the being. Sufis practice whirling to enter states of ecstasy, Christians sing, Jews say countless blessings, Muslims prostrate themselves in the direction of the divine. Giving, singing, dancing, loving: are all forms of prayer. Common attitudes of prayer are kneeling, touching the forehead to the ground, raising the arms, touching the heart.

Prayer doesn't come from the mind; it cannot be a thought. Prayer comes from the heart and addresses God, the divine, the spirit of oneness.

> *Whither shall I look when I praise Thee?*
> *Upward or downward, inward or outward?*
> *For You are the place in which all things are contained:*
> *There is no other place beside You: all things are in You.*
> *—Hermes*

WHAT IS MEDITATION?

*M*editation, like prayer, is a doorway to the being, but whereas the practice of prayer is to move toward the heart, the practice of meditation is to silence the mind. In the Eastern traditions a meditation is a technique used to attain to a state of inner emptiness in which individuality ceases to be a preoccupation and one merges with the very substance of existence—which is bliss.

There are many, many techniques of meditation, varying from the use of mantras, to a sensing of the body, or the witnessing of a particular gap in the breath. Meditation techniques have been used to develop groundedness as well as esoteric powers, and they come to us in forms as diverse as yoga and vipassana, activities such as chanting and spinning, and the old, old practice of listening, witnessing, or watching your breath.

In recent years, meditation has become a popular alternative to prayer. Perhaps because our minds have become so very overloaded, the practice of meditation—of stilling the mind—has become a practical necessity. For many, a time of meditation is a time to be alone, quiet, still. Spirituality today offers more and more choices for individual exploration and experimentation, and many of us are experimenting with meditation in the forms of Zen and Tibetan Buddhism, yoga, and the martial arts.

Meditation is related to medicine and is a deeply healing process that begins, in most forms, by closing the eyes and relaxing. From there, we are directed toward some aspect of the body, mind, or breath.

In the famous opening of the *Vigyan Bhairav Tantra* of Hinduism (c. 2500 B.C.E.) the God Shiva was asked by his consort Devi:

> *O Shiva, what is your reality?*
> *What is this wonder-filled universe?*
> *What constitutes seed?*
> *Who centers the universal wheel?*
> *What is this life beyond form pervading forms?*
> *How may we enter it fully,*
> *above space and time,*
> *names and descriptions?*
> *Let my doubts be cleared.*

And in reply, Shiva described for her 118 basic techniques of meditation—techniques that have continued to be the foundation for all modern meditation.

1

Radiant one, this experience may dawn between two breaths.
After breath comes in and just before turning up—the beneficence.

27

Roam about until exhausted and then, dropping to the ground,
in this dropping be whole.

33

Simply by looking into the blue sky beyond clouds, the serenity.

35

At the edge of a deep well look steadily into its
depths until—the wondrousness.

41

While listening to stringed instruments, hear their composite
central sound; thus omnipresence.

THE USE OF A MANTRA

In Eastern spiritual practices, it is recognized that the greatest impediment to happiness is the constant chatter of the mind. Only when the mind becomes still is it possible to experience the soul. One method of achieving this is to experience the hypnotic effect of repetition. We all know the effect of a lullaby. The use of a mantra is similar.

Mantras were developed as an aid to meditation. Specific words with specific vibrations help us transform the activity of the mind to a calmer condition where the mind is still, or even silent. You may have already discovered the basics of this technique without knowing what you were doing. Do you hum a tune or talk to yourself when you need to concentrate or to feel more at ease? Hypnotherapists use a form of mantra to get access to our unconscious states. Repetition, in the form of a mantra or a prayer, is like a subtle knock on the door that keeps us separated from the divine beauty of existence we were born into.

The frequently chanted mantra *Om Mani Padme Hum* encloses the phrase "the jewel in the lotus" between two symbols of sound, *OM* and *HUM*. The jewel in the lotus symbolizes the awakening of human consciousness — which is the jewel — out of the mind of man, as the lotus arises out of the mud.

Hindus say that the sound of a mantra is like the sound of the ocean. If you follow it, you will inevitably find yourself at the root of the sound that is the original soundlessness of the universe, the basic

element of existence. When we close our eyes and become silent, *OM* is the humming sound we hear.

Before the beginning of things, according to the Hindu tradition, Brahman (Sanskrit for the eternal, imperishable Absolute) pondered, "I am only one—and if I become many . . ." This pondering caused a vibration, which was the sound of *OM*, and creation was set in motion. This sound is the closest approach to Brahman that is possible, and the sacred symbol of *OM* has become emblematic of Brahman.

The vibration produced by chanting *OM* corresponds to the vibration that arose at the time of creation. *OM* also represents the four states of consciousness: the waking, dream, and deep sleep states, and the fourth state, the eternal state of blissfulness in which the self ceases to have identity and becomes one with existence.

The symbolic configuration of *OM* indicates that it has nothing to do with language. Christians hear this same sound as "amen," Muslims hear it as "amin." It is a sound that is attached to all prayers in the world's great religions.

THE IMPORTANCE OF
PRAYER AND MEDITATION

*P*rayer and meditation, in any of their many forms, remind us of what is most sacred to us. The practice of them empties us of all that is superfluous and fills us up with what is divine. We become more heartful, more aware, less complicated and fragmented, and more grounded; we are better able to live in balance and harmony in the world. Rather than reacting to things with anger or frustration, we become able to respond with awareness and love.

There are several different aspects of prayer and meditation which, apart from bringing us more in touch with ourselves, we often use in our daily lives.

When we need protection from fear or doubt, they work well to calm us, making space for us to contemplate and consider.

When we want to effect a change in our health or in a relationship, they can provide positive values and energy to negative situations.

When we want to find balance, harmony, or strength in our lives, the effectiveness of both prayer and meditation have been proven by centuries of use. They are now recognized by science as the greatest natural cures for all the collective maladies of stress and strain.

THE SPIRITUAL PATH

If you do not know the way, seek where His footprints are.
—Rumi

The spiritual journey begins when a deep longing arises to enter the mysteries of the unknown. This is often felt as a longing to experience God.

My father was a priest and as a young child I would sit in his church, soaking up the great silences, the hymns, and the prayers. I loved the richness of the deep velvety sense of devotion. These early experiences are something I have always remembered. Almost inevitably, as a young adult, I entered a time of deep inner turmoil and needed to find something that would give meaning to my life. My search began.

I left home and began meeting people who were asking themselves the same questions I was. We sought each other out, we passed books among ourselves, we drank tea, and we talked . . . sometimes all night long! The questions we were asking ourselves were, of course, the same questions that have preoccupied humanity as far back as we can go. Drawings left on cave walls, remnants of ceremony in burial places, the remains of ancient temples, all these give us an indication that when the human spirit was first emerging, it met with the great mystery. Questions of origin and belonging, of fear and courage, of life and death, have always been with us. They are the questions that lead us on, that guide our search.

MYSTICAL CONTEMPLATION AND
THE MYSTICAL BEAD AND THREAD

The most beautiful thing we can experience is the mysterious.
It is the source of all true art and science.
—Albert Einstein

The contemplation of the mysterious is a doorway to prayer. The word "contemplation" comes from the Greek word for a space marked out for devotion—a temple. A temple is a place wherein the divine is encountered. This can be anywhere—indoors, outdoors, a place intended for worship or one created in nature. The very body you live in is a temple.

In the ancient Hindu and Buddhist traditions temples are built in the shape of the top of the head with a topknot to which the energy of God can be connected. In the Christian traditions, the great cathedrals are similar in shape to the hands held in prayer. Temples, mosques, pyramids, and churches are all doorways to the divine and together with the rituals that are performed inside of them they hold keys to entering the holy or sacred states of being.

The great temple of our body is the basis for all temples. Within the body is the altar. With the sky and the unknown above, and the earth and all that we know below, our soul is the seat of all godliness. When we contemplate, we enter a temple. We behold the mysterious from within a place of awe or love; we contemplate the mysteries of the unknown from a place of humbleness and gratitude.

THE BEAD

Out of life comes death,
and out of death, life.
Out of the young, the old,
and out of the old, the young.
Out of waking, sleep,
and out of sleep, waking,
the stream of creation and dissolution
never stops.
—Heracleitus

As objects, beads have a particular beauty. They are round like the earth. They remind us of cycles and spheres, of seasons, of birth and death. Like the heavens they turn, like eyes they can see within and without. Because of their shape they have no beginning and no end. They are at once the container and the contained.

When they become devotional, beads become deeply symbolic. At their most utilitarian, they are among a family of objects that are called "apotropaion" or "designed to avert or protect from evil." "Eye Beads" protect us from the evil eye, and there are beads that protect the sailor from the sea and the lover from harm, beads that give us courage, prosperity, imagination, or good luck.

Joan Mowat Erikson in her book, *The Universal Bead* proposes that the resemblance between beads and the human eye are at the root at the significance of the bead.

"The eyes may be a basic clue to the elemental power
of rounded objects. . . . It is with the eyes that mother
and child communicate before speech develops, and the meeting
of the eyes serves as an adjunct to speech whenever language fails. . . .
We begin life with this relatedness to eyes; seeing protects us,
we feel secure when there is light. Eyes have been described as shining,
laughing, dancing, glowing, glaring, gleaming, like beads—and are,
like beads, colored blue, green, gray, brown, and golden.

It is very interesting that the early English use of the word "bead" was "prayer." In *The Faerie Queen,* Spenser says of an old woman:

All night she spent in bidding of her bedes,
And all the day in doing good and godly deedes.

The word "bidding" meant both making an offering and uttering a plea, meanings that are equally present in the concept of prayer. This earlier meaning of bidding is familiar in another archaic word "bedesman," a person who, for a consideration in a will, would regularly pray for the repose of passing soul.

THE THREAD

𝒪ur lives consist of a thousand and one incidents, and behind all those incidents is a connecting thread: the thread of our soul. Often we are unable to see it, and we forget its existence. We know of our suffering and our pain, our joys and our sorrows because they are everyday events. But when we look at our lives, when we search deep down within our beings, we see that there is a thread running inside. Within the deepest pain, within the greatest joy, when we are suffering and falling apart or happily goofing off, something holds us together.

Like beads strung along a thread, the events of our life contain meaning for us. Our soul is like the thread. It can either be seen as an intrinsic part of the string of beads, or separate from it. The soul, like the thread, is what gives shape and meaning to the events, or beads in life. This is the deepest symbolism of prayer beads.

Another aspect of the thread is that of the circle it makes. We circle an object—a maypole—as homage to the seasons, or we draw a circle around ourselves to ward off the power of witches and demons. We speak of going on our rounds.

Like everything in the universe, we go round and round. We are part of the continual revolving of the skies. Spinning, circling, revolving is an energetic impulse that centers. As every circle has a center, so does the human being. The center is as a core, a seed, a heart, or a hara. Sufi Dervishes engage in an ecstatic whirling that bears them upward. At the core of the circles they spin within is a lightness of being. This lightness of being is what we might call "heaven," "nirvana," or "bliss." It is akin to coming home, to finding our true nature, to knowing godliness within ourselves.

Part Two:
THE TRADITIONS OF PRAYER BEADS

---●---

We sometimes seek answers to our own questions of identity by looking back in time and piecing together a sort of continuum. We piece together various events, philosophies, and beliefs to give ourselves a broader understanding of who we are and also to add understanding to our perception of others. We enrich and enliven ourselves by acknowledging our roots, both mythical and real, the roots of our descendants and the roots of our shadows.

Observing others gives us great glimpses into ourselves. From what we observe, we can assimilate what is useful to us, and by doing so we change and grow.

In this section we will look at various traditions of using prayer beads. Their use goes way, way back in time. Archaeologists have found evidence of beads 40,000 years ago—a time that predates the emergence of cave paintings. Looking back to this time gives us an idea of the very earliest expressions of our spiritual world.

THE BEGINNINGS

$\mathscr{A}$rchaeologists have done much to uncover details of the lives of early man. The first glimpse of human culture, as we know it, is found in simple stonecutting tools that were made in East Africa 1.9 million years ago. These tools belonged to *Homo habilis*, an early ancestor of the human being that we know today.

As these early ancestors of ours evolved, cooperation began to grow between them, and settled communities arose. With community came the ideas of art and adornment—and beads.

Perhaps the earliest beads were gathered seeds and nuts that were pierced and strung, and thereby took on a new significance. We can only imagine our primitive forebears and the development of their spiritual and intellectual lives, but it is easy to guess that the seed and nut would be symbols of fertility, the cyclical seasons of nature, and the process of birth and death.

We can guess that as those early people found themselves in need of strategies to help cope with the power of the natural world, they devised ways to both protect and empower themselves, and that early forms of the bead were worn close to the body as amulets to protect and empower the wearer. Specific materials and shapes developed along with the desire to influence, either directly or indirectly, the major concerns of fertility, health, strength, and protection. Beads and amulets, we can be sure, accompanied rites of passage, rites of the hunt, rites of fertility, birth and death.

About 17,000 years ago, simple techniques had evolved for boring through and polishing soft pebbles and stone, giving rise to the search for more beautiful and stronger gems and metals. Techniques developed, and in graves dating from 7,000 years ago at a town called Varna in the Balkan region, beads have been found that were hammered out of gold. As civilization developed, sophisticated systems of commerce evolved, and man began to trade everything from concepts and ideas to raw materials. From the times of the great urban civilizations of the Euphrates and Nile valleys we have numerous examples of beautiful beadwork fashioned from materials gathered across great distances. Mesopotamian and Egyptian kings employed full-time jewelers, and bead making technology developed rapidly. Around 6,000 years ago, a substance called faience became the first mass-produced synthetic material to simulate precious stones. This led to the production of glass and popularized the technology of beadwork.

As metalworking advanced, beads were crafted from semiprecious and precious metals into a variety of shapes with many different textures. In ancient Egypt and Mesopotamia the earliest-known gold beads were formed into the shape of seeds, the age-old symbol of life.

PRAYER BEADS IN CONTEMPORARY RELIGIOUS TRADITIONS

The spreading, melding, and merging of religious concepts, and the evolution of our present-day traditions, is something that happened over centuries.

As far back as we can see, mankind has ventured abroad on the threshold of new discovery of unfamiliar lands. As he did so, people of one nation met people of another. People with one set of beliefs met people with other sets of beliefs. Ideas were exchanged, borrowed, and incorporated into existing traditions. We really have no way of knowing if the idea of prayer beads arose spontaneously in different traditions or whether the idea traveled forth from India, where scholars agree that the formal use of prayer beads originated. We do know that as far back as the eighth century B.C.E. the ancient Hindus were using them.

H I N D U I S M

*O*f the religious traditions alive today, Hinduism is recognized as being the oldest and perhaps the most embracing. The word *Hindu* is the early Persian pronunciation of the Sanskrit word *Sindu,* which means "river." The name stuck as the Persians brought back word of the people they had met in their early explorations of the Indus Valley.

During its early history, the people of India were isolated from the rest of the world by the great Himalayan mountain range. They had a peaceful agrarian culture and a profound understanding of the eternal nature of things with religious feelings based upon the earth and its fertility. From about 1500 B.C.E. these people began to be invaded by an Aryan race from the north, a nomadic people, oriented to Gods of the sky more than of the earth. The Aryans brought with them a religion based on oral texts known as *Vedas*, which are considered to be eternal truths. They were revealed to *rishis* or "seers" in states of deep meditation and consist of a large number of verses describing all aspects of spiritual knowledge. One of these series of Vedas—the Atharva Veda—gives explicit instructions on a wide range of formulas for different rites and traditions of folk belief, and ceremonies, rituals, and songs. It is in the Atharva Veda in about 800 B.C.E. that we have the first known mention of the use of beads for prayers. The beads they used are called *tulsi* beads and they are strung to make a *mala*. *Japa* is the practice of passing these beads through the

fingers while chanting a mantra, or sacred words.

> Japa *beads made out of tulsi or precious stones fulfill all desires.*
> *Those made in the shape of the tail of a cow or serpent offer*
> *even more auspicious results. One should not touch the* mala *with*
> *the second finger. Nor should one shake or swing his beads. One should*
> *change the direction of the beads on the thumb joint with the middle finger.*
> *One should never touch the beads with his left hand. Beads should not*
> *fall down from the hand. Those who are desirous of liberation, material*
> *enjoyment, or advancement of knowledge chant on the middle finger.*
> —*Hari-bhakti-vilasa (32)*

The next Veda gives rules for chanting

> *To be attentive, purification of the heart is required. This means*
> *keeping silence, that is, avoiding unfavorable talking. While chanting,*
> *one must affectionately remember the meaning of the mantra. Steadiness,*
> *patience, and attachment to chanting are all treasures of chanting.*
> —*Hari-bhakti-vilasa (33)*

It was the merging of two ancient cultures in early India, the early agrarian culture of the Indus valley with the Vedic religion of the Aryans, that has given us the tradition that today we speak of as Hinduism—a rich tradition with an extraordinary pantheon of Gods and Goddesses who reflect upon and act out the eternal aspects of the human condition.

One of the ancient stories of Hinduism and the use of beads tells of a visit that Indra made to Mt. Kailasa to see the great God Shiva. Indra found Shiva in deep meditation with his prayer beads. As he opened his eyes to greet Indra, he asked, "Indra! Why are you here? I know that there is no great trouble in the world so I know you have not come to ask me to fight with someone."

Indra replied saying, "It is true that I only visit Kailasa when I need you to fight, but at least this time it's not with a demon."

"What is the problem then?" Shiva asked.

"Well, I have just had a little argument with Narada. I said that you are the most powerful of all Gods, but Narada insisted that Vishnu is the more powerful."

Shiva said to Indra, "You see this *japamala* I am holding? Do you know what I am doing with it? Do you know what I am chanting?"

"I heard you chanting the name of Rama," Indra replied. (Rama is one of the many incarnations of the God Vishnu.)

"Yes," replied Shiva. "And you are asking me who is more powerful. If I am more powerful than Lord Vishnu, then He would be chanting my name. But it would never happen; it is I, Shiva, who chants the name of Rama."

The *japamala* that Shiva refers to is his string of prayer beads. It is one of the very early names given to them. Literally *japamala* means "a garland of roses" for in some instances the beads were made of dried and rolled up rose petals. *Japa* also means "whispering" or "murmuring."

Hindus use their *malas* in the chanting of a name or a symbol for God as in "Rama. Rama. Rama" or "Hari Krishna, Hari Rama"—two chants that have become familiar to Westerners. For a Hindu, the name of God is the same as the existence of God, so repeating a name of God is an invocation of that which is represented by the word. There are three types of *japa*: repetition out loud, repetition in the mind, and silent repetition with the lips.

The number of beads in a Hindu *mala* is traditionally 108, a number that gets its significance from their cosmology, which states that there are 108 dimensions, or elements of the universe. There are also 108 names for the sacred river Ganges, there are 108 Upanishads, and 108 names for both Shiva and Tara referring to the different manifestations of the eternal male and the eternal female, *and* there are 108 methods of meditation.

Another story that contributes to the history of the early *mala* tells of Shiva who, looking down at earth from his home on Mount Kailasa, wept when he saw the towering metropolis, Tripura, or Triple City. Tripura, a city conceived through man's technology, was a magnificent human creation that undermined the balance between the earth, the atmosphere, and the sky. Shiva's tears fell to earth in the form of the *rudraksha* seed and, having shed the implacable tear, Shiva drew his bow and unleashed his arrows at the Triple City, burning its demons and hurling them into the ocean.

Rudra is another name of Shiva, and *rudraksha* seeds are used in

the *malas* of many Hindus, reminding them of Shiva's compassion for the human predicament. The word *rudraksha* comes from the Sanskrit words *rud* or *rodden*, meaning "cry" or "crying" and *akshu* meaning "tears." *Rudraksha* literally means "the tears of Rudra." *Rudraksha* seeds have many healing qualities as well.

The stories of the gods and goddesses of Hindu mythology accompany an extraordinary legacy in the eternal search for truth. There are four ancient texts in Hinduism—Vedas (of which the earliest date back to 1200 B.C.E.), Upanishads, Ramayana, and Mahabharata (which includes Bhagavad Gita)—and they are incomparable in their depth and understanding of the human condition. They are the basis for Jainism, Buddhism, and Sikhism and have influenced not only Taoism in China but also some aspects of the monotheistic traditions of Judaism, Christianity, and Islam. As these early Indian traditions make their way into our Western lives there is no more absorbing venture than that of their discovery and understanding.

Hinduism speaks of meditation, karma, *brahma*, yoga, *bhakti*, guru; and as these concepts are incorporated into our language, there is no doubt that we grow richer and more tolerant.

The "peace and love" revolution of the seventies saw people embracing many aspects that were rooted in Hinduism. From the clothes that were worn to the books that were read, the East has been at the root of an enormous change, that continues today, in an age of tremendous spiritual upheaval.

B U D D H I S M

$\mathscr{B}$uddhism emerged at a time not so different from our own. It was a time of great material wealth and deteriorating morals. At the time of the birth of Gautama Buddha in 563 B.C.E., the priests or Brahmans of India had taken control of every aspect of life and demanded huge sums for the recital of religious rites. A strong movement among the youthful seekers of India was underway against them, and at the time of the enlightenment of Buddha, seven other enlightened mystics were teaching in the small state of Bihar in India. The names of six of these mystics are unknown; the one we do know is Mahavira, who became the twenty-fourth tirthankara and founder Jainism.

The story of Buddha's life has now become quite familiar to us. He was the son of a rich prince who had done his best to keep the child from seeing the suffering of the world. Inevitably though, the young Siddhartha discovered its existence and left home in search of that which does not grow old, get sick, and die. From here unfolds the story of Siddhartha Gautama's search to know himself. What he found, and the expression of his understanding, form the basis of Buddhism. In a great leap of understanding, Gautama Buddha took religion out of the hands of the priests and gave it to the individual, saying that the individual must make a personal endeavor to find his or her true nature.

Buddha's words and the stories of his life happened in a time when information was passed on in the form of songs or verses called

sutras, which in Sanskrit means "thread." In the Mokugenji Sutra of Buddhism we hear about a king who went to listen to Buddha. This king willingly embraced everything that Buddha said and wanted so much to bring the wealth of wisdom to his people, but there was serious famine and pestilence throughout his country. "My country is troubled and the people are terribly distressed and disheartened. They have so much work to do that I can't really feel easy about having them stop everything they are doing in order to practice your teachings. It is a painful position for me. What you say is so profound, but too vast to practice. Please teach me a simple exercise that I can pass on to my people."

Buddha instructed him:

"If you want to encourage them to eliminate earthly desires and to put an end to their suffering, tell them to make a circular string of 108 beads made from the seeds of the Bodhi tree and to keep it always with them. As they pass the beads one by one through their fingers they can say to themselves:

> *Buddham saranam gachchami*
> *Dhammam saranam gachchami*
> *Sangham saranam gachchami*
>
> *I take refuge in the Buddha*
> *I take refuge in the teaching of the Buddha*
> *I take refuge in the community of the Buddha*

This is known as the *trisharana* or "three jewels" of Buddhism and is said daily by devout Buddhists the world over. The words "take refuge" have a sense both of quenching thirst and of seeking understanding. People turn to Buddhism to begin a journey that will lead them toward themselves. The revolution in consciousness that Buddha brought about was the realization that every individual is responsible for his/her own state of being and transformation. Priests no longer stood as intermediaries between God and human beings.

The legends of Buddha's life and the message he gave have traveled throughout the East, influencing and merging with religious practices everywhere.

It was around 800 C.E. that Buddhism entered Tibet, where it blended with local customs and evolved into a rich tradition employing a large number of meditation techniques that also included prayer beads.

The Tibetan prayer beads, *trengwa*, are an elaboration on the Buddhist *mala* with beads of coral, shell, ivory, amber, turquoise, and other semiprecious stones on which Tibetans attach personal items such as keys, favorite ancestral beads, tweezers, and files. With the addition of "counter beads" they became capable of counting up to 10,800 prayers and as practices developed that were centered on continual chanting this was very useful.

Buddhist *malas* are generally made of 108 beads where the number 108 refers to the number of feelings or passions arising from the six

sensations of sight, sound, smell, taste, touch, and consciousness. Each of these six sensations is associated with pleasant, unpleasant, or indifferent feelings (18 feelings) and each of these feelings has two classifications—those that are attached to pleasure or those that are detached from pleasure (36 feelings). These 36 basic feelings are manifested through time—past, present, and future—giving us a total of 108 feelings.

In recent years Buddhism has penetrated the West where it is evolving into a living practice of meditation for thousands of people. Teachers and peacemakers have arrived from the Buddhist traditions not only of Tibet and Japan, but also Korea, Thailand, and Vietnam. Their influence is being felt more and more strongly not only in furthering the practices of meditation but also as new solutions are being looked at in issues of health, human rights, and world peace.

CHRISTIANITY

*C*hristianity, centering on the miracles of Jesus Christ, has had a profound influence over the emotional, moral, intellectual, and political climates in the West since its beginnings. With its roots in the Eastern border of the Mediterranean, Christianity, along with Judaism and Islam, emerged as a tradition of prayer. Based on a desire to follow the example shown in the figure of Christ, Christians seek godliness through prayer. The resurrection of Christ is an indication to the Christian that transformation is possible and that what is needed is a humble and a sincere heart. Christianity is a religion based on heartfulness, compassion, understanding. The miracles of giving, sharing, and humility are embraced as the foundation of the Christian journey.

In the early Christian traditions of Europe, which were deeply intertwined with Celtic practices, prayer beads were first used as talismans. Coral was thought to purify blood and prevent illness in children, and early paintings depicted the Christ child holding a string of coral beads.

By the eleventh century, the church hierarchy had decided that beads were better suited for counting devotions than pagan talismanic protection. Both the illiterate and those unschooled in Latin were assigned prayers to memorize and repeat using the prayer beads. These became known as "Psalters" or "rosaries." The medieval Church's position of stressing simplicity in personal adornment was met by women

wearing progressively more elaborate prayer beads, the only article of jewelry that was permitted to be beautiful. While they always carried rosaries, priests, monks, and nuns were forbidden the use of coral, quartz, or amber, because of their so-called "pagan" attributes.

In the mid-sixteenth century Pope Pius V decreed St. Dominic (1170–1231) as the official inventor of the rosary and it was at this time that the use of the rosary was sanctified.

The story goes that St. Dominic was so dejected by his failure to convert the Cathars to Christianity that he retired to a cave in the wilderness. After three days' penitential fasting and prayer, he collapsed, exhausted, and had a vision in which the Virgin Mary appeared to him accompanied by three queens and fifty maidens. She raised him up, kissed him, and quenched his thirst with milk from her chaste breasts. She then told him that "thundering" against heresy was not going to help, but rather that a gentle remedy against sickness was required. "Therefore, if you would preach successfully, preach my Psalter." She showed him the rosary that had the scent of roses, for the Virgin had brought them from her rose-garden in Paradise. Then she vanished.

The early Christian monks of Ireland greatly encouraged the regular singing of the 150 Psalms with the Psalter. They divided the beads into three sets of fifty, three being significant as the nature of the trinity. The people of Ireland were illiterate and knew no Latin, so they could not sing or recite the Psalms. They were given a single prayer that was to be repeated 150 times.

The word "rosary" is derived from the Latin word *rosarium*, or rose garden. The rose garden in medieval times was a place for prayers. For Christians the red rose grew to symbolize the blood of Christ and the white, the purity of the Virgin Mary.

Mary, the Virgin Mother, holds a very special place as the mother of Christ, or the aspect that gives rise to the incarnation of God in man. She is the embodiment of the female goddess and is fundamental to the spirit of compassion that is so essential in Christianity.

The connection between the Virgin Mary, the rose garden, and the rosary grew very strong in the art of the Middle Ages, in which Mary was often pictured sitting in a rose garden. So whereas the garden of Adam and Eve represents man's fall, the rose garden of the Virgin Mary represents the soul that gives birth to God in man. She has been referred to as the "rose of modesty," a "rose among thorns," the "mystic rose," "chaste rose," "rose of heaven," and "never-wilting rose." Dante calls her the "Rose in which the Word of God becomes flesh."

In today's rosary, fifteen large beads divide the rosary into "decades" or groups of ten. The small decade or Ave beads are used to say "Hail Mary" prayers and the large separator or paternoster beads are utilized in the "Lord's" and "Gloria" prayers. Each decade represents a subject or mystery in the life of Jesus and Mary.

The "Hail Mary" is a basic prayer in the Catholic tradition and arose in medieval times when Mary appealed to Christians in her resemblance to the disappearing goddess. The earliest form of "Hail

Mary" was the greeting of the angel Gabriel at Nazareth, according to St. Luke's gospel:

Hail Mary,
full of grace,
the Lord is with you.

With these words God told Mary, through the angel Gabriel, that she would bring Jesus Christ into the world. Over time the greeting given to Mary by her cousin Elizabeth was added:

Blessed are you among women
and blessed is the fruit of your womb.

Finally by the fifteenth century, the remainder of the prayer appeared:

Holy Mary, mother of God,
pray for us sinners now and at the hour of our death.

OTHER PRAYERS OF THE ROSARY

THE OUR FATHER OR LORD'S PRAYER

Our Father, who art in heaven, hallowed be Thy name;
Thy kingdom come; Thy will be done on earth as it is in heaven.
Give us this day our daily bread; and forgive us our trespasses
as we forgive those who trespass against us; and lead us not
into temptation, but deliver us from evil: for thine is the kingdom,
and the power, and the glory, for ever and ever. Amen.

GLORIA

Glory be to the Father, and to the Son, and to the Holy Spirit.
As it was in the beginning, is now, and ever shall be,
world without end.
Amen

THE APOSTLE'S CREED

*I believe in God, the Father Almighty, Creator of heaven and earth;
and in Jesus Christ, His only Son, our Lord; who was conceived by the
Holy Spirit, born of the Virgin Mary, suffered under Pontius Pilate,
was crucified, died, and was buried. He descended into hell;
the third day He arose again from the dead; He ascended into heaven,
and sits at the right hand of God, the Father Almighty; from thence
He shall come to judge the living and the dead. I believe in the
Holy Spirit, the Holy Catholic Church, the communion of saints,
the forgiveness of sins, the resurrection of the body, and life everlasting.
Amen*

HAIL! HOLY QUEEN

*Hail! Holy Queen, Mother of Mercy, our life, our sweetness,
and our hope. To you do we cry, poor banished children of Eve.
To you do we send up our sighs, mourning and weeping in this
valley of tears. Turn then, O most gracious advocate, your eyes of
mercy toward us; and after this our exile, show unto us the
blessed fruit of your womb, Jesus. O clement! O loving!
O sweet Virgin Mary! Pray for us, O Holy Mother of God.
That we may be made worthy of the promises of Christ.
Amen*

I SLAM

The recollection of God makes the heart calm
—Sura 13:28

He who recollects God among the negligent
is like a fighter in the midst of those who flee,
like a green tree in the midst of dry trees
—Qur'an 1:265

Today's Muslim tradition, along with the Christian and the Jewish ones, arises out of the desert of the Arabian Peninsula. With a common ancestor—the prophet Abraham—these three traditions of monotheism, although they have warred incessantly, are more related in spirit and zeal with one another than they are with the traditions arising out of India.

The roots of Islam begin historically with the Prophet Muhammad. As a young man, in the midst of rival claims about God from the Jews, Christians, and many polytheists in Arabia, Muhammad would go to Mount Hira near Mecca to search for the truth about God. It was there, in a cave on the mountain, that he was overwhelmed with a tremendous sense of God pressing upon him to recite.

"Recite what?" he asked.

"Recite in the name of your Lord who has created man . . ." and prayer was born in the heart of Muhammad. As time went on,

Muhammad continued to hear the voice of God (Allah) speaking to him and directing him and before long he arose as a leader in the Islamic world. His words were gathered by his followers in the Qur'an, meaning "recitation," which became the foundation of these people's beliefs. Traditionally the Qur'an is chanted, and its words are considered untranslatable because translation corrupts. Making the Word of God beautiful in Islam is both an act of worship and of thanksgiving, and explains the decoration in Muslim manuscripts and architecture.

The word "Islam" means both "peace" and "surrender" and a Muslim is one who lives life in surrender to God. Prayer is an act of inviting God into your heart. Allah had told Muhammad, "Remind people, for reminding benefits them" and he bids them to "celebrate Allah with abundant celebration." This prayer, this continual remembering, is called *Dhikr* and it has two forms—public and private. The public form is the *adhan*, the call for daily prayers that happens five times a day.

The private form is said using prayer beads which are called *tasbih*, *masbaha*, or *sibha* meaning "to exalt" or "to praise." The *tasbih* is made up of 99 beads divided into groups of three and separated with a special larger bead, or a tassel of gold or silk. The beads themselves are often made of the sacred clay of Mecca or Medina. With the passing of each bead through the fingers, an aspect of Allah or God is uttered.

For a Muslim, there are 99 attributes or "beautiful" names of God that can be uttered; however, none but the camel knows the 100th name, for it is not possible to utter the real name of God. It is said that the camel's scornful look of superiority comes because he knows the 100th name of God and refuses to tell.

The mystical aspect of Islam is called Sufism, and according to Sufi doctrine, when Absolute Reality decided to create the observable universe, it first differentiated itself into the Attributes that are assigned to these ninety-nine names. You can compare this to the rainbow of colors when a beam of white light is passed through a prism. As the light is focused and its rays made to intersect with each other, they produce different hues. Every creature or form is the locus of various divine names and attributes, and it is from this process that the manifestations of actions and temperaments upon a particular configuration of light unfold.

Well known to Muslims is the story of 'Ikrima, who asked his teacher 'Umar al-Maliki about *Dhikr*-beads. 'Umar answered that he had once asked his teacher Hasan al-Basri about it and was told: "Something we have used at the beginning of the road we are not desirous to leave at the end. I love to remember Allah with my heart, my hand, and my tongue."

Imam Suyuti recounts this story in one of his fatwas and at the end of it he comments: "And how should it be otherwise, when the prayer beads remind one of Allah Most High, and a person seldom sees prayer beads except he remembers Allah, which is among the greatest of its benefits."

NINETY-NINE NAMES OF GOD

1. AL RAHMAN

The Compassionate, or Beneficent, showing compassion to all creatures.

2. AL RAHIM

The Merciful. He who bestows mercy on the Faithful.

3. AL MALIK

The King, or Sovereign Lord, whose dominion is clear from imperfection.

4. AL QUDDUS

The Holy, or Sacred, who is pure and clear from adversaries.

5. AL SALAM

Peace or Tranquility, or The Source of Peace.

6. AL MU'MIN

The Faith-Giver, or Guardian of the Faith. The Trusted.
The One who has witnessed for Himself that He is God;
and has witnessed for His believers that they are truthful
in their belief that He is God.

7. AL MUHAYMIN

The Preserver, or Protector, especially of trust.

8. AL 'AZIZ

The Mighty, The Glorious, or The Victorious.
That which is not defeated.

9. AL JABBAR
The Compelling. That which cannot be disobeyed.

10. AL MUTAKABBIR
The Imperious, The Proud, being clear from the attributes
of the creatures and from resembling them.

11. AL KHALIQ
The Creator. The One who brings everything from
nonexistence into existence.

12. AL BARI'
The Maker or Evolver, planning and leading creatures
through all the stages of their development.

13. AL MUSAWWIR
The Shaper or Fashioner, molding and giving form to things.

14. AL GHAFFAR
The Pardoner or Forgiver.

15. AL QAHHAR
The Destroyer or Subduer.

16. AL WAHHAB
The Bestower, being generous in giving plenty without any return.

17. AL RAZZAQ
The Provider, The Sustainer.

18. AL FATTAH
The Opener, opening the way to all developments.

19. AL 'ALIM
The Omniscient or All-Knowing.

20. AL QABID
The Constrictor, making things difficult.

21. AL BASIT
The Expander, making things easy.

22. AL KHAFID
The Humbler, providing humility.

23. AL RAFI'
The Exalter. The One who raises whomever
He wills by His Endowment.

24. AL MU'IZZ
The Honorer, bestowing honor, giving esteem to whomever He wills,
hence there is no one to degrade Him.

25. AL MUDHILL
The Degrader or Abaser, degrading whomever He wills,
hence there is no one to give him esteem.

26. AS SAMI'
The All-Hearing.

27. AL BASIR
The All-Seeing, The Discerning.

28. AL HAKAM
The Judge.

29. AL 'ADL
The Just, meting out everything in due measure and
due proportion so that not the slightest deviation or imbalance
exists in the universe.

30. AL LATIF
The Sublime, The Subtle, or Gentle One. He who is generous,
wonderful, too fine to be seen by the eye, and whose actions are
not easy to comprehend.

31. AL KHABIR
Awareness, Knowing the Truth of Things.

32. AL HALIM
The Lenient, Gentle, or Patient One.

33. AL 'AZIM
The Mighty, The Magnificent, or Great One, deserving
the attributes of Exaltment, Glory, and Extolement.

34. AL GHAFUR
The Forgiver or All-Forgiving.

35. AL SHAKUR
The Appreciative, The Grateful, The Thankful.

36. AL ʿALI
The High or The Lofty, The Lord On High.

37. AL KABIR
The Great, The Big.

38. AL HAFIZ
*The Protector or Preserver, protecting all things, especially
His divine Word (the Qur'an), for all time.*

39. AL MUQIT
*The Nourisher, The Sustainer, The Maintainer. Of the three principles:
creation, continuity, and destruction, this supplies the second.*

40. AL HASIB
The Reckoner, or Giver of Final Satisfaction.

41. AL JALIL
*The Majestic or Sublime One, attributed with greatness
of Power and Glory.*

42. AL KARIM
The Generous, The Bountiful, being clear of abjectness.

43. AR RAQIB
The Watchful.

44. AL MUJIB
The Responsive, responding to prayer.

45. AL WASI'

The All-Embracing, The Omnipresent, The Knowledgeable.

46. AL HAKIM

The Wise. The source, possessor, and dispenser of all wisdom.

47. AL WADUD

The Loving, The Bestower of Love, and The Beloved.

48. AL MAJID

*The Most Glorious, having perfect Power, Compassion,
Generosity, and Kindness.*

49. AL BA'ITH

*The Raiser or Resurrector, creating life and giving new
life to that which is apparently dead.*

50. ASH SHAHID

The Witness.

51. AL HAQQ

Truth or Reality.

52. AL WAKIL

The Trustee, the name by which we put our trust in God.

53. AL QAWI

The Infinitely Strong.

54. AL MATIN

The Firm, withstanding and resistant.

55. AL WALI
The Friend.

56. AL HAMID
The Praiseworthy.

57. AL MUHSI
*The Enumerator or Counter. The source of divine measure
and proportion.*

58. AL MUBDI'
*The Creator, The Originator, having created the entire
universe and all the worlds.*

59. AL MU'ID
*The Restorer. Whatever is taken away, can also
be given back or returned.*

60. AL MUHYI
The Lifegiver, giving life to all living things.

61. AL MUMIT
The Slayer, or Destroyer, bringing death.

62. AL HAYY
The Living or Alive. Neither is He born, nor does He die.

63. AL QAYYUM
*The Everlasting or Self-Subsisting, being eternally erect,
wakeful, and watchful.*

64. AL-WAJID

*The Embodier or Finder. Whatever is to be found in this world,
He gives corporeal existence to.*

65. AL MAJID

*The Union, The One, The Unique. All multiplicity finds its
combination in Him.*

66. AL-WAHID

The Noble, The Illustrous, The Glorious.

67. AL AHAD

*The One, The One Without a Second, not in terms of a mathematical
sequence of numbers, but of "That of which there is no other."*

68. AS-SAMAD

*The Eternal-Absolute, The All-Sufficient. He who is relied
upon in matters and reverted to in one's needs.*

69. AL QADIR

The Able, The Capable.

70. AL MUQTADIR

The Powerful, that from which nothing is withheld.

71. AL MUQADDIM

The Hastener or Expediter.

72. AL MU'AKHKHIR

The Delayer.

73. Al Awwal
The First, Before Everything, whose existence is without a beginning.

74. Al Akhir
The Last, The Remainder, whose existence is without an end.

75. Az Zahir
The Manifest, The Apparent.

76. Al Batin
The Hidden.

77. Al Wali
The Governor, owning and managing things.

78. Al Muta'ali
The Most Exalted, being clear from the attributes of the creation.

79. Al Barr
The Benefactor or Source of All Goodness.

80. Al Tawwab
The Acceptor of Repentance.

81. Al Muntaqim
The Avenger.

82. Al 'Afuw
The Forgiver or Pardoner.

83. AR RA'UF
The Merciful or Compassionate.

84. MALIK AL MULK
The Possessor of the Kingdom of God.

85. DHU 'L-JALAL WA 'L-IKRAM
Lord of Majesty and Bounty. The One who Deserves to be Exalted, and Not Denied.

86. AL MUQSIT
The Equitable. Economy also derives from this name, whence the divine economy, which is equitable and in just measure.

87. AL JAMI'
The Uniter or Gatherer, uniting all things in Himself.

88. AL GHANI
The Wealthy or Self-Sufficient, not needing that which is created.

89. AL MUGHNI
The Enricher, The Bestower, satisfying necessity.

90. AL MANI
The Supporter.

91. AL DARR
The Distresser, The Afflictor, bringing on adversity.

92. AL NAFI'
The Beneficent, helping and healing.

93. AL NUR
The Light.

94. AL HADI
The Guide.

95. AL BADI
The Originator or Incomparable, having created the creation
without any preceding example.

96. AL BAQI
The Eternal or Everlasting, for whom the state
of nonexistence is impossible.

97. AL WARITH
The Inheritor, to Whom everything returns.

98. AL RASHID
The One Who Guides or Rightly Guided, the name bestowed
upon all prophets, saints, sages, and true masters.

99. AL SABUR
The Patient, the source of all patience, and that which endures.

J U D A I S M

The origins of Judaism, like those of Christianity and Islam, lie in the deserts along the eastern Mediterranean, in countries that today are known as Israel, Jordan, Palestine, and Syria. With the flourishing kingdom of Egypt to the south, Mesopotamia to the east, and the land of the Hittites to the north, the world of these early peoples was a natural corridor for both traders and invading armies that consisted of nomadic tribes searching for and fighting to retain a collective identity. The result has been that each of these three traditions arose to unite its peoples with the strength of the conviction that they had been chosen by a unifying God.

The sacred writings of the Jews are contained in the Torah, which contains the first five books of the Bible and 613 commandments given by God to Moses, who led the Israelites out of slavery. Ten of these commandments are shared with Christians and form the principles of creating a stable and civilized society. The rest of the 613 commandments include the moral teachings and rules of ritual and hygiene.

Jerusalem was made the capital city of the Jews by King David, the first of their great kings. His son Solomon built the temple that housed the Arc of the Covenant, their national religious relic. This temple was destroyed by the Romans in 70 C.E., and the rituals that

could no longer be performed there were replaced by prayer, and it was prayer that became the unifying spiritual container for the people.

The use of prayer beads did not become a part of Jewish practice, but they do use a prayer shawl called a *Talith*, which must have four tassels, and be made of blue and white silk. This shawl has six hundred fringes, eight strings, and five knots and is similar in some respects to prayer beads.

A *Talith* contains two Hebrew words; *tal* meaning tent and *ith* meaning little. Thus, these early people had a "little tent" representing a private sanctuary where they could meet with God. This prayer shawl or *Talith* was pulled up over one's head, forming a tent within which one could chant and sing the Hebrew songs, and call upon Elohim, Yaweh, Adonai. It was an intimate, private time, totally focused upon God.

For Jews the *Talith* or *Talis* is a religious symbol, a garment, shroud, canopy, or cloak that envelops one both physically and spiritually, in prayer and celebration, in joy and sorrow. It is used at all major Jewish occasions: circumcisions, bar or bat mitzvahs, weddings, and burials. It protects the scrolls of the Torah when they are moved. The dead are wrapped in it when they are buried. The bride and bridegroom are covered with the canopy of the prayer shawl.

And the LORD spake unto Moses, saying, speak unto the children
of Israel, and bid them that they make them fringes in the
borders of their garments throughout their generations, and that
they put upon the fringe of the borders a ribband of blue:
and it shall be unto you for a fringe, that ye may look upon it,
and remember all the commandments of the LORD, and do them;
and that ye seek not after your own heart and your own eyes,
after which ye use to go a-whoring: that ye may remember,
and do all my commandments, and be holy unto your God.
I am the Lord your God, which brought you out of the land of Egypt,
to be your God: I am the Lord your God.
—Numbers 15:37-41

Judaism is a tradition of prayers, rituals, and blessings that bring the sacred into daily life by practicing reverence in everyday acts. The Jewish path is often called the Blessing Path and it is a tradition that teaches and expects its people to count 100 blessings a day. In doing so, everything is imbued with the divinity of God.

E Y E   B E A D S

"Eat thou not the bread of him that hath an evil eye,
neither desire thou his dainty meats; for as he thinketh in his heart,
so is he: eat and drink, saith he to thee; but his heart is not with thee.
The morsel which thou hast eaten shalt thou vomit up,
and lose thy sweet words."
—*Proverbs 23:6-8*

"Then, with incantations, she invoked the Spirits of Death,
the swift hounds of Hades who feed on souls and haunt the lower air to
pounce on living men. She sank to her knees and called upon them,
three times in song, three times with spoken prayers.
She steeled herself with their malignity and bewitched the eyes
of Talos with the evil in her own. She flung at him the
full force of her malevolence, and in an ecstasy of rage she plied
him with images of death."
—*The Greek poet Apollonius of Rhodes writing of how*
the sorceress Medea destroyed the giant Talos with her gaze.

*O*ne of our most pervasive beliefs, going way back to Paleolithic times, is that eye contact with a particular human, demon, or malevolent force can harm people and their property or afflict them with evil emotions.

Human feelings are communicated through the eyes. Through them we express friendliness and trust, and through them too we reveal our hatred and malice. There is a malignant power in the glance of hate that is often felt to be the essence of evil itself. The phenomenon surrounding the malicious glance of hate is called the "evil eye," and since early times, people have devised magic means to protect themselves from its attack. Amulets, carved stones, and talismans have been devised in extraordinary variety to meet this particular age-old need for protection against the evil eye.

The simplest and most powerful protection against the evil eye is the bead—a symbol for the eye itself. In Egypt and India the eye has become a mystical symbol of great potency, going far beyond the talismanic quality of the eye bead and representing the ability to see and to know. It is, after all, the ability to see clearly that dispels ignorance and darkness. It is also in the nature of the eye that it perceives light.

Eye beads are beads of various colors, shapes, and materials that are decorated with, or which have intrinsic to their natural colors, one or more spots resembling eyes. The earliest known examples of eye beads are Egyptian ones made of painted clay. With the invention of glass, a drop of a darker color could be pushed into the matrix of the already formed bead and after that, techniques were devised to raise the eye from the surface of the bead with bands of different colors, thus making it protrude. The variety was enormous and the techniques continually changed as new skills were developed.

WORRY BEADS

*W*orry beads can be seen in the hands of people all over Greece and although they were inspired either by the Islamic *tasbih* or the Christian rosary, their purpose is not prayer.

The Greek word for worry beads is *komboloi,* and it is derived from the word *kombos,* meaning knot or a large number of knots, and *loi,* meaning a group that sticks together. Some people think that worry beads were adapted from the prayer strands used by the monks of Mount Athos in northern Greece, who used a prayer strand of woolen knots tied onto a string. Another theory suggests that worry beads traveled across the Aegean Sea from Asia Minor. It is thought that when the Turks occupied Greece after the fall of Constantinople, from 1453 to 1821, the rebellious Greeks used to mock the occupying Turks and their use of beads for prayer by devising a set of their own. The beads were then simply assimilated into the Greek culture as it was realized that the momentum of passing the beads through the fingers took the mind off worrying.

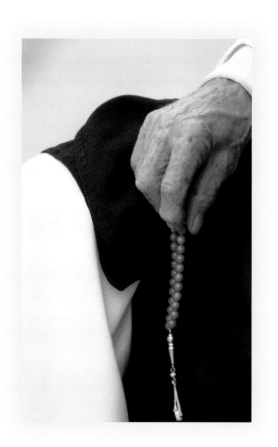

Part Three:
YOU AND YOUR PRAYER BEADS

●

Having looked at the traditions and uses of prayer beads, it is now time to contemplate your own. The beads in this box are a simple set of prayer beads made of 108 sandalwood beads with a single yellow wooden bead where the knot is tied. They are here for you to experiment with. The pouch they are in is a good place to keep them when you are not wearing them. These beads are yours to befriend. Take them in your hands and become familiar with them, for the journey you are about to embark upon is a rich and ancient one.

At some point, you may want to make your own set of prayer beads. This is an experience that can be at the same time wonderfully creative and personally enhancing. The process by which you find, choose, and string together your beads is a small journey in itself.

O rosary! O rosary! O great calculator!
You are the essence of all power.
In You are found the four goals
{material prosperity, pleasure, morality, and liberation}.
Therefore grant me all success.
-Mahanirva na-Tantra (from the Vedas of Hinduism)

THE BEADS IN THIS BOX

The string of beads that comes in this box consists of 108 sandalwood beads with a single yellow bead to cover the knot where the string is tied. The components of your prayer beads all have some meaning.

Both Hindus and Buddhists have traditionally used the number 108 in their malas. It is tremendously significant because of its ability to be divided into many different numerical relationships and therefore contains an abundance of ideas. Duality (2) and trinity (3), directions (4), and senses (6), are among the many aspects that are parts of the number 108. It also expresses a divine relationship between the planets, the moon, and the cosmic ages of time.

Sandalwood, of which your beads are made, has a history which goes back 4,000 years. Its ancient use in religious ceremonies is record-ed in both Chinese and Sanskrit texts. The oil of the sandalwood tree has bactericidal properties and was imported by the Egyptians for

embalming because it aids in preservation. Sandalwood is universally used as incense for it eases the passing between spiritual dimensions or states. It has a delicious woody smell with a relaxing effect, a smell which will linger when your beads are removed.

The single yellow bead, which hides the knot, is known in Hindu and Buddhist traditions as the "guru bead." The word *guru* is Sanskrit for "teacher" and has a very deep meaning. If you are to arrive in a strange city and want to find a particular street there are two approaches to take. One is to try your luck and search it out on your own, the other is to ask a native. The guru is that guide in the spiritual dimensions and can be perceived as a presence outside of yourself or as an inner quality. It is this quality of your prayer beads which is most transcendental. As you use them you will find in them a relationship to your very deepest longings.

Yellow was chosen as the color of the bead that covers the knot because it is the color of the sun and as such it represents the light by which we see. When the sun rises we wake up, when it sets we go to sleep. The sun becomes a reminder of our sleeping nature and of our capacity to climb out of sleep and to seek that which is eternal, that which no longer sleeps, that which knows no death. The color yellow is a reminder to wake up.

So, your simple set of beads already has a lot of significance, and this significance will become even richer as you bring to it your own understanding and incorporate in it your own experiences.

Take your beads in your hand. This is the first step in acquaint-
ing yourself with them. Play with them for a while. Allow your fingers
the pleasure of fondling or caressing the beads. Move the beads slowly
through your fingers and sense the slight gap between the bead and the
string. Rub the beads with the motion that is used to create heat and
start a fire. Jingle them in the cup of your hands. Listen to them. Look
at them. Put them in your pocket for a while, and then around your
wrist.

Once you have "made friends with" your beads, you can get
down to developing a deeper relationship with them, working out a
practice that will enhance their significance for you. The practice that
you develop will depend, in part, on your own spiritual leanings. You
may want to use them ritually as a part of a daily prayer. You may
want to use them more casually as an occasional reminder of a feeling
or an emotion of reverence. Whatever your approach, allow your beads
to remind you of that which is sacred. Without such a reminder life
can become quite perplexing. Keep in touch with the divine, the
mysterious, the wonder, and your life will be rich.

Any one of the following can be used as an approach to developing your own practice or remembrance:

REPETITION

Decide upon a short prayer or a mantra that you can repeat over and
over. One word—OM—will do, or a very simple prayer—Love is
God. Of course you can use a prayer or a mantra of any length; but try

something short to begin with. Repeat the phrase in whichever way is easy for you—aloud, with the movement of your lips, or silently—and with each repetition, pass a bead through your fingers. Try this at first for a short while, maybe a minute or two. The idea is to let the repetition work as a distraction to pull your mind away from whatever it is currently working on. If you can learn to create a small gap in the process of your mind, you can then find a way to slip through that small gap into a space that is more present, more silent, more meditative, more prayerful. Simply pay attention to what stirs in your heart as you repeat your prayer, and let yourself move away from the dominion of your mind.

SLOWING DOWN

Begin by holding the beads in your hand and passing the beads through your fingers. Don't try to say a prayer, simply pay attention to sensing your fingers at work. Feel the beads. Feel your fingers moving over and around them. Sense into them and try to feel them from the inside. Withdraw your attention from the beads and bring it to the inside of your arm. Bring it back out again to the beads. Touch a bead and bring your whole attention to what is happening. Slow down. Linger with your fingers around the bead and allow yourself to come to a stop. Move out of your mind and into the slowness. When you are ready, move on to the next bead. Go as slowly as you can and enjoy the feeling.

W H O   A M   I ?

Use your beads to help answer the question "Who am I?". With each bead that moves through your fingers, find an answer. Go round the thread a couple of times finding different answers to the question. Eventually you will come to a point where there is nothing but a simple, very powerful experience of being.

You can create many variations on this theme. With each bead you can sense into a different body part, with each bead you can remember a person you love, with each bead you can bring your attention to yourself.

Experiment with your beads. If you grow tired of them, put them someplace special so that when you pick them up again they will remind you to look within. Your beads will reflect back to you all the care that you give them. They can become very meaningful for you in your spiritual quest or journey or in the desire to bring a calmness to your simple, everyday life.

KEEPING A PRAYER JOURNAL

If you keep a journal, you already know its benefits. If you haven't had the experience, you might try keeping one as you begin the practice of using beads, for a journal is a place where you can watch things unfold. It is a place where you can let go of your inhibitions and express your feelings with freedom. You can explore yourself and your relationship to the world and your friends around you. You can note and have a place to keep prayers or phrases that touch you or that you enjoy saying to yourself.

Find a place where you can be comfortable and alone with yourself for a while. It is best if you can set aside enough time to complete whatever process happens. I find this kind of time to be very important. Without it, I tend to get so involved in things outside of myself that I forget to spend the time that I need in order to come back home.

There are of course as many ways to begin a journal as there are to begin your day. You can contemplate and give it shape before you begin, or you can jump right into it and see how it unfolds. If you are not used to writing, you might begin by collecting prayers you like. One thought is to assign a page of your journal to each bead, and to each bead a prayer. As you are using 108 beads, find 108 prayers and give each one a page. Start there and see what happens.

A journal doesn't have to be written with words—you can collect pictures or dried flowers; it doesn't have to be written on paper—you can create your pages on your computer. Maybe you, like some people I know, prefer to have a drawer or a box that is dedicated to this process.

You may find that you return from time spent with your journal with insights that influence your life. Whatever happens, allow. The process is for you to enjoy. All life, in the ancient Hindu tradition, is a *leela* : a play, a mystery to be lived—not one that can be solved.

RITUALS AND YOUR BEADS

*T*he tendency to create rituals in our lives stems from the time when everything was perceived as divine. It is one of the greatest losses in our modern times that in our haste to get somewhere quickly, we have forgotten about the sacred; in our attempts to satisfy our needs, we have turned toward the profane and lost track of the godliness inherent in every moment. Rituals bring us back to ourselves and kindle a sense of enjoyment and pleasure. They help us to pass through the events of our lives.

Let's look at a ritual we all know very well—that of giving a birthday present. The birthday of a loved one approaches. It is a special day and stands out from those that go before or after it. We contemplate our friend and search for and find something that will be a token of our love. We wrap it so that it can be opened with some ceremony. We find a card that expresses the importance of our relationship. We wait, anticipating the special moment when our gift will be opened and we can experience the delight of the other. This is a tremendous ritual involving our hearts and our hands in the great act of giving.

Your beads can be a gift to yourself. Create a ritual acknowledging your receptivity to them. This will deepen their significance. You might use incense, light a candle, or play music that you feel is appropriate when you first put them on. If you do, you will find that using your prayer beads will begin to signify to you that life is the prayer you live.

The very use of your beads may become a ritual for you. Allow the sight and touch of them to kindle a feeling of deep reverence. Allow them to awaken your prayerful heart. Allow yourself to remember your divinity.

Just to be is a blessing.
Just to live is holy.
-Rabbi Abraham Heschel

CONSIDER CREATING YOUR OWN
SET OF PRAYER BEADS

*F*inding or making beads and stringing them is an experience many of us enjoyed in our childhood. The delight intrinsic to the act of stringing beads is similar to any creative act. As bead by bead the thread is filled up, the strings tied, the circle completed, a deep sense of satisfaction emerges. The experience of creating something whole out of many parts is deeply symbolic. Like the events of our lives, the beads are strung upon the thread. Like words in a sentence or notes in a song, individual beads have a beauty intrinsic to themselves; bound together they form something greater than the parts.

You may consider making your own beads. Originally, beads were made by simply boring a hole through a seed, wood, or seashell. Any organic material that you can drill a hole in can be used to create beads.

Because it is so common and malleable, clay is another good medium for beads. When wet, clay beads can be handcrafted or pressed into molds to form a variety of shapes. Patterns can be etched onto them or a glaze of color applied. Then the beads can be fired and strung.

Here is a recipe for making beads from rose petals.

ROSE PETAL BEADS

1/3 cup wheat flour

1 tbs. salt

2 tbs. water

3 cups rose petals

Round toothpicks

1. Mix flour, salt, and water to make a stiff dough.

2. Cut rose petals into tiny pieces, then crush by rolling between your palms.

3. Mix as many rose petals into your dough as possible without making it crumbly.

4. Shape small amounts of dough into beads.

5. Push round toothpicks through the center of each to make holes.

6. If desired, scratch designs into beads.

7. Allow to dry a few days; remove toothpicks before dough gets too hard.

   Makes enough for one strand.

You can make your own strings of beads by purchasing semiprecious stones or wooden beads and stringing them yourself. Beads come in a great variety. If you decide to buy beads, consider the aspects of color, shape, and size along with whatever symbolic or spiritual attributes they might have. Choosing beads is an opportunity to discover new and interesting aspects of yourself.

You can create a few different sets of beads in different colors and sense for yourself how you respond to their different qualities. This is a wonderful process of self-discovery.

If you decide to string your own beads, take the opportunity to go deeper than superficial likes and dislikes. If you choose green, contemplate for a while the significance the color has for you.

You will also need to decide on how many beads to string — an odd or an even number — and how long a strand you want to make. Some people use elastic thread to string their beads, giving more flexibility but less strength. You can also attach a tassel or an amulet to the point where the knot is tied. Here again, the choices you make may be influenced by the beliefs you hold and if they do, then respect those choices, for anything that deepens your relationship with the mysterious is a great gift to yourself.

OUR EVOLVING SPIRITUAL PRACTICES

In the last hundred years or so, we have seen a tremendous shift in our spiritual practices. Traditions that have been passed from parent to child for centuries are now changing. As new frontiers in communication open up, there is suddenly a wealth of information which was previously available only to the scholar or the intensely curious. The universe is at our fingertips. Television, movies, books and magazines with wonderful photographs, the Internet and interactive software, all of this has contributed to an absolutely new awareness of the world we live in. Sacred texts have been translated and made available to all, and everything is open to interpretation and speculation. Ancient practices of yoga and the martial arts have entered the arena of body care and physical fitness, and we can even learn them on TV. Traditions that once depended on deep commitment are now embraced with casual understanding. The rebel, who we once thought of as the anarchist or the insurgent—seeking out answers to his questions through the arduous task of going against prevailing beliefs or searching in forbidden texts—is now a normal student. To question authority, to argue with elders, to challenge belief, to search out and investigate new frontiers are all accepted modes of behavior. And while the rebel has always had a respected place in the annals of history, spiritual rebelliousness has taken on a totally new meaning for us in recent years.

We are standing at the threshold of a new age in which all sorts of possibilities are open to us. As the search to know ourselves continues, we continue to find new ways to meet the divine and to express our gratitude. One of these ways, one of great beauty, is the one you will now begin to discover for yourself—the ancient use of beads for prayer.

Do Beads Have Power?

*A*ll organic substances have subtle energetic properties. Crystal, well known for its electrical properties, is the basic element used in silicon computer wafers and has long been used—as are many substances—as an aid to amplifying and projecting positive energy. When misused, subtle energies can attract negative energy.

I remember a time in India when a Westerner I knew returned from Tibet wearing a *mala* he had purchased that was made from the bones of someone who had died. Now the Tibetans consider these beads to be very sacred, but within a few weeks this man became very ill, and it wasn't until he heeded the good advice of a friend to throw the *mala* into the sea that he began to get better.

It is important to understand that when you wear or use any object with some spiritual or symbolic significance, it is natural that you will be affected by it on some level. Perhaps you will not notice it much; perhaps you will feel it strongly.

Another aspect of the substances used for beads is the colors they radiate. Colors are similar to musical notes where one note in its relation to other notes creates a chord that is either pleasing or unpleasing, soothing or disturbing. Color works in a similar fashion, influencing the electromagnetic centers of our bodies and the corresponding etheric, emotional, and mental systems. These centers are all documented in Asian medicine and Hindu and Buddhist literature.

Simply wearing prayer beads will not produce any power in and of itself, but they must be used with thought and respect, for there is always a possibility that they may interfere with your own kinetic system of body-mind. As human beings we exist in many dimensions, and we all have different strengths and weaknesses. As well as the subtle energies that exist in the world around us, we are privy to the secrets of our unconscious, and as easily as joy and happiness can emerge from our depths, so too can our demons. If you use an object that is not new, an object that you have found or purchased second-hand, it is really important to be aware that it may or may not carry energies you can resonate with. That is why, in all spiritual traditions, objects used for any technique of prayer, devotion, or meditation are best if they are received as gifts. The energy of giving is the most healing energy we know. It is strongly transferable and deeply nurturing. Beads that have been given to you specifically for prayer are unquestionably the most desirable. If you go out to buy your own beads (and it is far better than getting them from a catalog) let your senses do the work. Respect your impulses and allow yourself to have the ones you really want.

CARE OF YOUR BEADS

$\mathcal{Y}$our beads deserve some special care. They reflect whatever you bestow upon them, so if it is love you give, it will be love you remember.

The string you use will eventually break with use. Even though this is a natural process, the moment it occurs is often seen to have some deep personal relevance. If your string breaks at an auspicious moment, it is important to give yourself the time to restring the beads with a sense of import. It is deeply symbolic and nurturing to do so.

Most often, the string breaks due to normal wear and tear, and it is wise to remove your beads before going to bed or during heavy physical activity. Generally, the attitude toward this breakage is (in the words of Buddha) that "all things are subject to dissolution, decay, and change."

It is better to keep them close to you and not to pass your beads around to others, as your subtle relationship with them may change. Keep them off the ground, as is true with all sacred objects, including books and other ritual instruments.

It is helpful to oil the beads from time to time, especially if you are wearing them close to your skin. Best are oils with very little smell or one that you find complementary to sandalwood. You can enhance the smell of your beads with rose, ylang-ylang or bergamot for example, but be aware that as they warm up with your body heat, the beads will release the aroma of whatever oil you use.

As with all special things, it is nice to keep them in special places. Whether it is on an altar you have made or in the sachet in which they have come, your beads will contain their energy if you are careful where you put them. One of the very strange things about objects we hold to be sacred is that they respond in an indescribable way to the way in which we treat them.

A FEW FINAL WORDS ABOUT
YOUR PRAYER BEADS

There are many, many ways you can become acquainted with yourself. Using prayer beads is one of them. Experiment with what you have read in these pages and please don't take anything too seriously.

Take your beads in your hands and let them speak to you. Cooperate with them and let your prayerful heart create a dance with them. Let your beads become a part of your song to existence; let them become an invocation or a call to God.

Remember, it doesn't matter what your spiritual leaning is. Perhaps you will use your beads to find a calmer space inside, or perhaps you will use them to activate your longing to know who you really are. Treat your beads with respect and allow them to reflect back to you the inner richness of your being. Prayer beads have a magic about them. In some uncanny way they lead you on, lead you in.

Existence unfolds in many ways and the doors that open to a prayerful heart are both mysterious and wondrous. It has always been so.

Remember yourself. Remember to sing and to dance. Remember that a joyful heart is a prayerful heart and that a prayerful heart is a blessed one.

The greatest journey we can embark upon is the one that leads to our interior—the vast, vast world, with many doors, many aspects, great richness, and a wonderful tradition. Let the steps you take be remembered in the use of your prayer beads. Take them with you as you go and let your journey be an uncharted one. Feel yourself like a bird in the sky with no footsteps to follow. Abandon yourself to the great freedom of discovering who and what you really are.

SELECTED BIBLIOGRAPHY

Arnold, Edwin. *Pearls of the Faith or Islam's Rosary*. Boston: Roberts Brothers, 1883.

Bowker, John. *World Religions: The Great Faiths Explored and Explained*. New York: DK Publishing, Inc., 1997.

Coles, Janet and Robert Budwig. *Beads: An Exploration of Bead Traditions Around the World*. New York: Simon & Schuster, 1997.

Daniélou, Alain. *The Gods of India: Hindu Polytheism*. New York: Inner Traditions International, 1985.

Dubin, Lois Sherr. *The History of Beads from 30,000 B.C. to the Present*. New York: Harry N. Abrams, 1987.

Erikson, Joan Mowat. *The Universal Bead*. New York: W.W. Norton & Co., Inc., 1969.

French, R.M., trans. *The Way of a Pilgrim; and, the Pilgrim Continues His Way*. San Francisco: HarperSanFrancisco, 1991.

Hanayama, Shinsho. *The Story of the Juzu*. San Francisco: Bureau of Buddhist Education, 1962.

Kunz, George Frederick. *The Curious Lore of Precious Stones*. New York: Dover Publications, Inc., 1971.

Mizuno, Kogen. *Buddhist Sutras: Origin, Development, Transmission*.

Tokyo: Kosei Publishing Co., 1982.

Osho. *The Book of Secrets: The Science of Meditation*. New York: St. Martin's Griffin, 1998.

Parrish-Harra, Carol. *The Aquarian Rosary: Reviving the Art of Mantra Yoga*. Tahlequah, Ok.: Sparrow Hawk Press, 1988.

Patton, Cornelius Howard. *The Rosary: A Study in the Prayer-Life of the Nations*. New York: Fleming H. Revell Company (no date).

Schimmel, Annemarie. *Mystical Dimensions of Islam*. Chapel Hill, N.C.: The University of North Carolina Press, 1975.

Smith, Huston. *The World's Religions: Our Great Wisdom Traditions*. New York: HarperCollins, 1991.

Thurman, Robert A.F. *Essential Tibetan Buddhism*. New York: Harper-Collins, 1995.

Van der Sleen, W.G.N. *A Handbook on Beads*. York, Pa: Liberty Cap Books, 1973.

Wilkins, Eithne. *The Rose-Garden Game: The Symbolic Background to the European Prayer-Beads*. Victor Gollancz, Ltd., 1969.

Winston-Allen, Ann. *Stories of the Rose; The Making of the Rosary in the Middle Ages*. University Park, Pa: The Pennsylvania State University Press, 1997.

ACKNOWLEDGMENTS

Grateful acknowledgment is made for permission granted to reproduce images in the text.

PAGE VI: *Early Heian Portrait of Gonzo.*
© *Burstein Collection/Corbis*

PAGE VIII: *Prayer Beads.* © *Corbis*

PAGE 4: *Mongolian Monks.*
© *Brian Vikander/Corbis*

PAGE 7: *Albrecht Duerer (1471-1528).*
Portrait of his father with rosary.
© *Alinari/Art Resource.*

PAGE 10: © *Mary Evans Picture Library*

PAGE 12: *Three Peasant Women
in a Village Church. Wilhelm Leibl,*
© *Kunsthalle, Hamburg.*

PAGE 14: *Prayer Beads, Niger.*
© *Paul Almasy/Corbis*

PAGE 16: *Bodhidharma in Meditation.
Hakuin.* © *Eisei Bunko Foundation, Tokyo.*

PAGE 20: *Ajanta cave frescos Bodhisattvas,
India, 200 B.C.E. – 400 A.D.*
© *Philip Baud, www.anthroarcheart.org*

PAGE 23: *Muslim man in prayer.* © *Corbis*

PAGE 24: © *British Library, London.*

PAGE 27: *Shrine to Gaea at the
foot of Mt. Parnassus, Greece.*
© *Philip Baud, www.anthroarcheart.org*

PAGE 28: *Das Jungste Gericht, Fra Angelico,
c. 1431. Museo de San Marco, Florence.*
© *AKG Photo LibraryDas.*

PAGE 32: © *Robert Harding*

PAGE 34: *Sumerian woman discovered
during the excavations at Ur.*
© *Mary Evans Picture Library, London.*

PAGE 38: *Krishna and His Consort, Rukmini.*
© *Corbis*

PAGE 40: *Krishna temple, India.*
© *Philip Baud, www.anthroarcheart.org.*

PAGE 43: *Belur Temple sculptures, 12th century,
Karnataka, India.*
© *Philip Baud, www.anthroarcheart.org.*

PAGE 45: *Ganesh on Lotus, c. 1720.*
© *British Museum, London.*

PAGE 48: *Gulvihara rock sculptures,
Buddha in Meditation.*
© *Philip Baud, www.anthroarcheart.org.*

PAGE 51: *Dalai Lama, London, 1999.*
© *Reuters/Ian Waldie/Archive Photo.*

PAGE 54: *Irish penitent.*
© *Mary Evans Picture Library, London.*

PAGE 56: *Madonna in the Rose Garden.
Stefan Lochner (1405-1451).*
© *Scala/Art Resource.*

PAGE 62: *Ubudiah Mosque.* © *Corbis*

PAGE 65: *The third orthodox khalif, Uthman,
seated with Koran and rosary.* © *Victoria and
Albert Museum, London/Art Resource.*

PAGE 78: © *British Library, London.*

PAGE 81: *Jewish man praying.* © *Corbis*

PAGE 85: *Worry Beads.*
© *Francoise de Mulder/Corbis*

PAGE 89: © *British Museum, London.*

PAGE 92: © *British Library, London.*

PAGE 97: *The Venerable Bede of Jarrow.
12th century British manuscript illumination.*
© *British Library, London.*

PAGE 98: *The Birthday. Marc Chagall,*
© *Metropolitan Museum of Modern Art, NY*

PAGE 106: *Donovan, New York, 1969.*
© *Terry Thompson/Archive Photo.*

PAGE 109: *Prayer Beads*
© *Ric Ergenbright/Corbis*

PAGE 114: © *British Museum, London.*

PAGE 117: *Avalokiteshvara. From Dunhuang,
c. 910.* © *British Museum, London.*

Photographs on pages 3, 15, 86, 94, 103, 113:
© *Amy Ray.*